Printed in the United States of America
by G&R Publishing Co.

Published By:

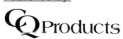

507 Industrial Street
Waverly, IA 50677

ISBN-13: 978-1-56383-343-4
ISBN-10: 1-56383 343-3
Item #3626

Cookie Bouquets

For Celebrations!

Create Your Own Gifts & Centerpieces

Delicious Designs

Table of Contents

Getting Started

Celebrate any festive occasion with one of these bright and cheerful cookie bouquets. They make the perfect gift or centerpiece for birthdays, special events or holidays. Use the no-fail recipes beginning on page 56 for easy edible bouquets. You may also use your own favorite recipes, pouches of cookie mix, or ready-to-use refrigerated cookie dough and icings. However, follow these tips for the best results:

- Reduce or omit baking powder from your cut-out cookie dough recipes to achieve clean cuts and nice edges.
- If using a pouch of sugar cookie dough, follow the package instructions for cut-out cookies.
- If using refrigerated sugar cookie dough, blend some powdered sugar or flour into dough before rolling out on a surface covered with additional powdered sugar.
- Always make a few extra cookies in case of breakage or decorating mistakes. This also allows you to add cookies to your container as needed for a full appearance.
- Cookies may be baked ahead of time and frozen (unfrosted) for several weeks. For best results, ice the cookies and assemble bouquet the same day it will be served.

Make each bouquet unique by interchanging the suggested types of cookies and icings. For example, prepare the birthday bouquet with lemon cookies instead of chocolate cookies, or use chocolate-flavored crispy peanut butter treats to make the Splish Splash Pool Party centerpiece. Make every celebration sweet and memorable!

Gather Some General Supplies

These supplies may be purchased in kitchen shops, craft stores, supermarkets or the baking and craft sections of discount stores. (Basics like scissors and foil won't be repeated in bouquet instructions.)

- **Food-safe containers (at least 3″ deep)**
- **Florist foam or Styrofoam ("foam")**
- **Knife to trim foam**
- **Scissors and decorative scissors**
- **Tape**
- **Waxed paper, aluminum foil and parchment paper**
- **Colored tissue paper**
- **Nonstick cooking spray**
- **Quart-size, heavy-duty zippered plastic bags**
- **White lollipop and cookie sticks (4″, 6″, 8″)**
- **Wood popsicle or craft sticks (4½″)**
- **Toothpicks**
- **Food coloring (Gel or paste coloring is recommended.)**
- **Ready-to-use decorating frostings and icings in plastic tubes and/or bottles: writing icing or gel, white cookie icing, black and red decorating icing**
- **Bent icing knife or offset spatula**
- **Rolling pin, sleeve and pastry cloth**

Preparing the Base

An important part of any cookie creation is choosing a fun container to enhance the theme. Containers should be at least 3" deep, food-safe and heavy enough to support the weight of cookies on stems without tipping. Look for flat sturdy bottoms and wide openings for easy assembly. Choose colors and trims that complement your cookies. Thrift stores, craft stores and your own closets are great places to find the perfect containers, and paint can provide a fresh look to old ones.

In some bouquets, crisp cereal treats are shaped with hands, molded in a pan or pressed into a container to hold the stems. After the cookies are removed, you can enjoy this edible base.

In other bouquets, non-edible Styrofoam or florist foam is used. The foam should fit into the container snugly when covered. To cut foam to the correct size, press the container's opening against foam to make an outline. Use a knife to cut out the shape, ½" inside the outline. Test the fit and trim foam as needed, until it fits down into container, about ½" below top edge. Cover foam with foil and then follow the bouquet instructions. Colorful tissue paper, shredded paper or small candies can be used to cover the foil.

Plan your arrangements based on the type and size of your container and cookie cutters. Use the photos for ideas, and then make the bouquets your own by choosing stem lengths and placements that work for your creations.

Choosing and Attaching Flower Stems

In most cases, wood craft sticks, toothpicks and white paper lollipop or cookie sticks are inserted into cookie dough shapes *before* baking. The sticks should extend about halfway up each cookie. Once cookies are baked and cooled, the stems should support the cookies securely. For cake balls, stems are inserted after they are shaped but before chilling or decorating. Basically, the heavier the cookie, the sturdier and shorter the stick should be. Large, heavy cookies may need thick cookie sticks or 2 stems.

In forward-facing bouquets, cookies at the front of an arrangement need shorter sticks. Those in the back need longer sticks. Sticks that are too long may be cut to the desired length. If in doubt, start with long sticks and carefully trim them with pruning shears or a serrated knife when assembling the bouquet. Hold the cookie and stem securely while trimming.

When inserting the stems into a base, handle them underneath the cookie. Push stems down firmly and slowly, stopping often to check appearance of arrangement. Push them far enough to obtain good support. Do not push stems all the way down until you are sure about placement. Make a toothpick starter hole through tissue paper or foil as needed. To adjust cookie positions, handle cookies by the sticks or unfrosted edges.

Happy Birthday!

Any birthday celebration will be
extra special with these chocolate
cut-out cookies decorated with
bright shiny icing.

You will need:

- Container (Sample uses a sturdy open cardboard box, 7″ square and 3″ deep.)
- Gift wrap paper
- Styrofoam
- Chocolate Cut-Out Cookie Dough (recipe on page 57)
- Cookie cutters (two sizes of gifts and party hats, 3″ and 5″; 3″ circle or balloon)
- 1¼″ round medicine bottle
- Royal Cookie Icing (recipe on page 59)
- Gel food coloring (neon purple, orange and green; classic red, blue and yellow)
- White lollipop sticks (4″, 6″, 8″)
- Toothpicks
- Curled ribbon or shredded paper to match wrapping paper

To Begin…

1 Prepare container. Wrap outside of box as if wrapping a gift, folding paper over open edges and taping securely to inside of box. Cut foam to fit into container snugly; wrap with foil and press into container.

2 Prepare cookies. Prepare Chocolate Cut-Out Cookie Dough using recipe on page 57. Roll out chilled dough to a thickness of about ⅜″.

- Cut these shapes with cookie cutters: 3 to 5 each of 3″ party hats and gifts, 3 circles, and 1 each of 5″ party hat and gift.
- Use the medicine bottle to cut out 13 small circles.
- Place cookie shapes on lightly greased or parchment paper-lined baking sheets, allowing space between cookies for sticks. Place similar sizes on each sheet.
- Cut 1″ off two 8″ lollipop sticks. Insert the 7″ sticks into the bottom of the largest gift and hat. (If these cookies seem too heavy, use 2 sticks in each cookie for added support.) Insert an 8″ stick into 2 balloons. Insert a 4″ stick into remaining balloon. (If desired, re-shape dough circles slightly with hands to resemble balloons.) Insert 8″ sticks into 2 smaller gifts. Insert 4″ sticks into remaining smaller gifts. Insert 4″ and 6″ sticks into smaller hats as desired.
- Insert a toothpick into each small circle for the "Happy Birthday" letters.

- Bake at 350° for 10 to 14 minutes or until cookies are set and just beginning to brown. Let cool on baking sheets for 2 minutes; transfer to waxed paper to cool completely.

3 Prepare and apply icing.

Mix one batch of Royal Cookie Icing using recipe on page 59.
- Divide icing between 4 bowls. Tint 1 bowl neon purple, 1 bowl neon orange, and 1 bowl neon green, stirring well. Leave the remaining icing white. Spread purple icing on 1 large gift. Spread orange icing on 1 small gift and 1 small hat. Spread green icing on 1 balloon, 1 small gift and 1 small hat. Spread white icing on each small round cookie. Cover bowls and reserve remaining icing for step 4 below.
- Mix a second batch of Royal Cookie Icing and divide between 3 bowls, reserving a few spoonfuls of white icing for piping in the next step. Tint 1 bowl blue, 1 bowl red and remaining bowl yellow plus neon orange. Spread blue icing on 1 balloon. Spread red icing on remaining balloon, 1 small hat and 1 small gift. Spread yellow-orange icing on the large hat and remaining small gifts and hats.

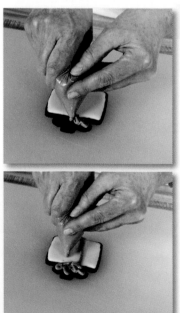

4 Prepare and apply piped icing.

Thicken the remaining colored and white icings in each of the bowls as directed for piping on page 60. Spoon each color of icing into a separate plastic bag and cut off one small corner of each bag. Pipe contrasting colors on the iced cookies, using photo for sample color combinations.
- To make bows on gifts, pipe lines back and forth on the top of each gift. Pipe several vertical

lines from bow to bottom of gift for a wide "ribbon."

- To finish party hats, pipe lines back and forth on top tassel as shown. Add polka dots and/or wavy or straight diagonal stripes on icing, using multiple colors as desired.

- Pipe a thin wavy reflection line of white icing on each balloon.

- Pipe a blue letter on each small round cookie to spell "Happy Birthday" as shown.

5 Put bouquet together.

Plan arrangement using photo as a guide. Curl long pieces of ribbon and cut them into shorter sections. Tie one piece around the stick on each balloon cookie. Push sticks firmly into foam, making starter holes with toothpick if needed. Scatter remaining curled ribbons over base to cover foil.

Variations: *Change the colors to match specific celebrations, such as using red, green, white and gold for a December celebration. Change the letters to reflect the theme, such as "Merry Christmas" or "Happy New Year."*

Celebration Suggestions...

Birthday, Retirement, Congratulations, Farewell or say, "Life is a party!" or "Hats off to you!"

This basket of sugar cookie flowers
is quick and easy to make because
colored sugars and candy sprinkles
provide the decorations.
No icing required!

You will need:

- **Container (Sample uses a round woven basket, 6″ in diameter and 4½″ deep.)**
- **Styrofoam**
- **Green tissue paper**
- **Ivory shredded paper**
- **Perfectly Tender Sugar Cookie Dough (recipe on page 57)**
- **1 egg white**
- **White lollipop sticks (4″, 6″, 8″)**
- **Colored decorating sugars (blue, red, green, yellow, pink)**
- **Rainbow candy sprinkles or M&M candies**

To Begin...

1 **Prepare container.** Cut foam to fit snugly into basket. (You may also use a Styrofoam ball that fits into basket with center of ball slightly higher than edge of basket.) Wrap foam in foil and cover in green tissue paper. Press into container. Scatter shredded paper on top.

2 **Prepare and decorate cookies.** Prepare Perfectly Tender Sugar Cookie Dough using recipe on page 57. (You will need a partial batch for this bouquet; use remaining dough for another bouquet or additional pinwheel flowers.) Divide dough into two portions and shape each into a rectangular disk, lightly flouring both sides. Chill dough for 2 hours.

- On a generously floured surface, roll one disk of dough at a time into a 6 x 12″ rectangle about ¼″ thick.
- Using a ruler and pizza cutter, cut dough into 3″ squares. Place squares on ungreased or parchment paper-lined baking sheets, allowing space between cookies for sticks. Make 12 to 16 squares. If desired, make several smaller squares for smaller flowers.
- In a small bowl, beat egg white with 1 tablespoon water. Brush surface of each dough square with beaten egg white.

- Lightly press about 1½″ of lollipop stick into bottom center of each square.
- Sprinkle colored sugar generously over each square. Make a variety of colors such as pink, green, blue, red, and yellow. Colors may also be combined.

- With pizza cutter, cut the dough diagonally from each corner to within ½″ of square's center.
- Fold alternating corners of the square to the center to form a pinwheel, overlapping the dough at the center and pushing down gently at center to seal corners.
- Press candy sprinkles or a single M&M in the center of each pinwheel.
- Bake for 10 to 13 minutes or until cookies are set and tips just begin to brown. Let stand on baking sheet for 2 minutes; transfer to waxed paper to cool completely.

3 **Put bouquet together.**
Plan arrangement using photo as a guide. Push flower stems (sticks) into foam base, starting with the tallest flowers at the back, or near the center, and working forward. Place some flowers on each side of the basket handle.

Variations:

- Use red and green decorating sugars to make a bouquet of poinsettia flowers for Christmas parties. Arrange them in a holiday container.
- Use school colors for an end of the school year party or spring sports celebration.

Celebration Suggestions...

Valentine's Day, May Day, Mother's Day, Get Well, Congratulations, Thank You, Family or Class Reunion, Bridal Shower, Spring or Summer Celebration or say, "You make my world spin!"

Talk About Love!

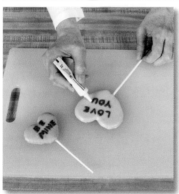

Prepare any cut-out cookie recipe listed on pages 56-57. Roll out dough to a thickness of ⅜″. Use heart-shaped cookie cutters in several sizes to cut at least 12 heart cookies. Insert 4″, 6″ or 8″ white lollipop sticks as desired. Bake at 350° for 8 to 12 minutes.

Prepare a double batch of Royal Cookie Icing using the recipe on page 59. Divide icing between several bowls and tint each bowl a different color to imitate the colors of "conversation heart" candies (pink, purple, orange, green and yellow). Leave one portion white. Place cookies on waxed paper. Thin icings slightly and spread icing over each cookie, allowing it to drip over edges until coated; let dry for 5 to 10 minutes. Move cookies to fresh waxed paper to dry completely, about 1 hour. Use red writing icing to pipe Valentine's Day messages on each cookie using upper case letters; let dry. Arrange cookies in a flower pot with a foil-covered foam base. Sprinkle conversation heart candies over foil.

Fun messages to include: UR KIND, BE MINE, MY BABY, SO FINE, LOVE YOU, BE GOOD, BE KIND, YOU RULE, YOU ROCK, UR SWEET, BEST FRIENDS, MY BABY, KISS ME, BE TRUE, TRUE LOVE, and CUTIE PIE.

Celebration Suggestions...

Valentine's Day, Engagement, Anniversary, Bridal Shower, Grandparents' Day or any "love" occasion.

Celebrate the arrival of spring and
the Easter bunny with this bouquet
of two-layer cut-out cookies featuring
a subtle lemon flavor.

You will need:

- **Container** (Sample uses a pink basket, 8″ long, 5½″ wide and 3″ deep.)
- **Styrofoam**
- **Green Easter grass** (or pastel-colored petite mints or M&M candies)
- **Lemon Sugar Cookie Dough** (recipe on page 56)
- **Cookie cutters** (3¼″ egg; 4″ bunny head; 3″ circle; 3½″ hatching chick; 3¼″ tulip and flower with petals; 2¼″ and 3½″ butterflies; 4″ hopping bunny; optional 3½″ cross)
- **White lollipop sticks** (4″, 6″, 8″)
- **Buttercream Frosting** (recipe on page 60 using lemon flavoring)
- **Gel food coloring** (colors of choice)
- **Ready-to-use decorating icing** (black)
- **Candy sprinkles** (orange, white, pink)

To Begin . . .

1 **Prepare container.**
Cut foam to fit basket. Wrap foam in foil and place into basket with top of foam just below top of basket. Spread Easter grass or candies over foil.

2 **Prepare cookies.**
Prepare Lemon Sugar Cookie Dough using recipe on page 56. Roll out chilled dough to about ¼″ thickness. (Cookies will be paired up before baking to make a double layer.)

- With cookie cutters, cut these quantities and shapes: 12 eggs, 2 bunny heads, 2 circles, 4 hatching chicks, 8 tulips, 2 to 4 flowers with petals, 2 butterflies of each size, 2 hopping bunnies and 2 optional crosses. Place 1 cookie of each pair on lightly greased or parchment paper-lined baking sheets, allowing space between cookies for the sticks.

- Place 1 stick on each cookie, with end just past the middle. Place sticks at different angles on eggs so they will tilt in various directions when assembling bouquet. Set matching cookies on top, lining up edges. Lightly

press cookies together. Place longest sticks (8″) on most flowers, 1 butterfly, bunny head and optional cross. Place 4″ sticks on eggs, circle, small butterfly and hopping bunny. Cut several sticks to

continued

2½″ lengths for chicks. Place 6″ sticks on remaining flowers. (Use any remaining dough for another bouquet or additional cookies.)

- Bake at 350° for 9 to 12 minutes until just beginning to brown. Remove from oven and let cool on baking sheets for 2 minutes; transfer to waxed paper to cool completely.

3 Prepare and apply frosting.

Prepare Buttercream Frosting with lemon flavoring using recipe on page 60.

- Spread plain untinted frosting on the bunny head, large circle (bunny's body), hopping bunnies and egg portion of hatching chicks; let dry.
- Divide remaining frosting between 4 small bowls. Tint 1 bowl yellow, 1 pink, 1 purple and 1 blue (or other colors as desired). Mix well. With an offset spatula, spread yellow frosting on both chicks. Spread different colors of frosting on eggs, flowers, butterflies and optional cross, using photo as a guide. Let dry.

4 Prepare and apply piped details.

Thicken remaining icing in each bowl as directed for piping on page 60. Place each color into a separate plastic bag and cut off one corner.

- Using photo as a guide, pipe designs on eggs and butterflies with different colors and patterns, such as zig-zags, dots and loops.
- Outline tulips with matching icing. Outline chick's egg with yellow icing.

- To make bunny's face, pipe pink icing on each ear as shown. Pipe a pink nose and mouth. Press pink sprinkles into frosting on each side of nose for whiskers. Use black decorating icing and a small round tip to draw eyes.

- Turn the large circle into the bunny's body by drawing 2 pink paws on front.
- Outline hopping bunnies with contrasting frosting. Pipe a black eye on each bunny. Pipe a pink nose, whiskers and mouth on bunny heads. Press white sprinkles on bunny's tail.

- Pipe a black eye on each chick and press 2 orange sprinkles on frosting to make each beak.

5 Put bouquet together.

Plan arrangement using photo as a guide. Press stems through foil into foam, moving Easter grass as needed so stems can be inserted easily. Place the tallest cookies toward the back first and work forward, placing shortest stems in front. To put the bunny together, slide stem of bunny head partway into foil and then push stem of round cookie (body) down in front of head until cookie touches foil. Adjust bunny head so it overlaps body slightly.

Celebration Suggestions...

Easter, Springtime or say, "Eggs-cellent Job!", "You're hopping now!" or "Bloom where you are planted."

Welcome Baby!

The arrival of a new baby is worth celebrating! Make this sweet bouquet filled with about 2 dozen iced sugar cookies. Glazed alphabet cookies adorn the cookie "blocks."

- Container (Sample uses a white oval basket, 9″ long, 5″ wide and 3″ deep.)
- Styrofoam
- White tissue paper
- Sweet Cut-Out Sugar Cookie Dough (recipe on page 56)
- Cookie cutters (3″ buggy; 3½″ bottle; 3¾″ and 1½″ circles for bib; 3½″ bear; 3″ duck; 3½″ footprint; 1½″ to 4″ hearts and stars; 2″ alphabet letters)

- Wood craft or popsicle sticks
- White lollipop sticks (4″, 6″, 8″)
- Toothpicks
- ½ C. powdered sugar
- 1 to 1½ T. Milk
- Royal Cookie Icing (recipe on page 59)
- Gel food coloring (yellow, green, blue, red or pink, purple)
- Pastel M&M candies (or petite mints)

To Begin . . .

1 Prepare container.

Cut foam to fit into container snugly; wrap with foil and white tissue paper, and then press into container.

2 Prepare cookies.

Prepare Sweet Cut-Out Sugar Cookie Dough using recipe on page 56. Roll out chilled dough to a thickness of ⅜″.

- Make a paper block pattern, 3 x 3⅜″. Place pattern on dough and cut out 4 blocks, using a pizza cutter to cut around pattern.
- Cut these shapes with cookie cutters: 1 footprint, 3 each of bottles, buggies, hearts and stars, and 1 each of teddy bear, duck and bib. (*To make a bib, cut out a 3½″ round cookie and use a smaller round cutter to remove a section from the top.*)
- Roll dough slightly thinner and cut out letters to spell "BABY."
- Place cookies on ungreased baking sheets, allowing space between cookies for sticks. (Omit sticks on footprint, 1 duck, 1 small heart and all letters.)
- Insert a wood craft stick into the bottom of each block cookie. Insert 8″ lollipop sticks into bib, 2 stars, 1 buggy and 1 bottle. Insert 6″ sticks into 1 small heart and 1 bottle. Insert 4″ sticks into bear, 1 duck, 1 heart and 1 buggy.

- Cut several 4″ sticks in half. Insert the half-sticks or toothpicks into remaining cookies.
- Bake at 350° for 8 to 12 minutes. Remove from oven and let cool on baking sheets for 2 minutes; transfer to waxed paper to cool completely.

3 Prepare alphabet letters.

Prepare a simple glaze by mixing powdered sugar with milk. Mix until smooth and thin enough to drizzle. Holding each alphabet cookie along edges, dip top and edge of cookie into glaze to coat; let excess drip off. Set cookies on waxed paper, glazed side up. Sprinkle with pink (or blue) colored sugar while still wet. Transfer cookies to fresh waxed paper to dry for 1 hour.

---

4 Prepare and apply icing.

Mix one batch of Royal Cookie Icing using recipe on page 59. Spread white icing on each block. While still wet, press 1 sugared alphabet letter on each block; let dry.

- Divide remaining icing between two bowls. Tint 1 bowl yellow and the other bowl green. Spread yellow icing on ducks, footprint and 1 star. Spread green icing on bear, 1 buggy and bottle.
- Thicken remaining yellow and green icings for piping, as directed on page 60 and place into separate plastic bags; set aside.
- Mix a second batch of icing. Divide between 4 bowls. Tint 1 bowl blue, 1 bowl pink and 1 bowl light purple. Leave the remaining bowl white.

- Spread blue icing on 1 buggy, large star and bottle. Spread pink icing on 1 bottle and 2 hearts. Spread purple icing on bib and 1 star, buggy and heart.
- Thicken remaining icings for piping, as directed on page 60 and place each color into separate plastic bags; set aside.

5 Add piped details. Cut off one corner of each plastic bag as directed on page 60.
- Using the photo as a guide, pipe blue icing "stitches" around each block and bib.
- Write baby's name or "Cutie" on the bib or star in white icing.

- Pipe details in contrasting icings on remaining cookies as desired, such as wheels on buggies, outlines, polka dots and facial features. Let dry.

6 Put bouquet together.
Plan arrangement, using photo as a guide. Insert craft sticks with block cookies first, alternating heights slightly and making starter holes with toothpick. Arrange other cookies around the blocks, with tallest cookies in the back. Sprinkle M&Ms over tissue paper. To finish bouquet, set cookies without sticks on the base. Fill in empty spaces with additional M&Ms.

Celebration Suggestions...

Baby Shower, Baby's Birth or Adoption, Christening, Pregnancy or Baby Announcement, or Baby's First Birthday.

Aboard the
Circus Train

Perfect for any children's party,
these iced sugar cookies
travel around an edible
two-layer cereal base packed
into a round container.

You will need:

- 3 x 5" notecard
- Round container (Sample uses 12" round plastic container, 3" deep.)
- No-Bake Crispy Peanut Butter Treats (recipe on page 59 using butterscotch and milk chocolate chips)
- Sweet Cut-Out Sugar Cookies (recipe on page 56)
- Cookie cutters (5 to 7 different animals, 3" to 4" tall; 2 people, 5" to 7" tall; 2" letter "L")
- 1¼" round medicine bottle

- White lollipop sticks (4", 8")
- White cookie sticks (6")
- 6 candy canes (6" or larger)
- Royal Cookie Icing (recipe on page 59)
- Gel food coloring (black, yellow)
- Ready-to-use decorating icings with round and star tips (red, blue, yellow, orange, green, purple, pink, black)
- ½ C. ready-to-use chocolate frosting in piping bag fitted with a small round tip

To Begin...

1 **Prepare paper pattern.**
With scissors, round off the edges of note card to make a paper pattern for the circus train cars; set aside.

2 **Prepare container.**
Grease container with nonstick cooking spray. Using the recipe on page 59, prepare one double batch of No-Bake Crispy Peanut Butter Treats with butterscotch chips. With buttered hands, press mixture firmly into container. Chill in freezer while preparing a second double batch of no-bake treats with milk chocolate chips. Firmly press second layer on top of chilled first layer. Chill for at least 30 minutes.

3 **Prepare cookies.**
Prepare Sweet Cut-Out Sugar Cookies using recipe on page 56. Roll out chilled dough to a thickness of ⅜".
- Measure container to determine how many train cars and animals will fit.
- Place paper pattern on top of dough and cut out 5 to 7 train cars, using a sharp knife to cut around the pattern.

- Place on ungreased baking sheets, allowing space between cookies for sticks. Cut 1 (4″) stick in half for each train car. Insert 2 short sticks into a long edge of each car, leaving approximately 2″ of space between them.
- Use the medicine bottle to cut 2 round wheels for each train car. Place on ungreased baking sheet without sticks.
- Cut these shapes with cookie cutters: 1 of each animal shape, 1 clown, 1 ringmaster and 2 "L" shapes. Place

  animals and people on ungreased baking sheet allowing space for sticks. Insert 4″ lollipop stick into the bottom of each animal and clown. Insert 8″ stick into bottom of ringmaster. Place the "L" shapes, back to back, on top of ringmaster's head to make a top hat, pressing edges together to finish shape.
- Bake at 350° for 8 to 11 minutes. Remove from oven and let cool on baking sheets for 2 minutes; transfer to waxed paper to cool completely.

---

4 **Prepare and apply icing.**
Mix one batch of Royal Cookie Icing using recipe on page 59. Ice cookies in desired colors, or as follows:
- Spread white icing on train cars, clown, ringmaster's shirt and zebra; let dry.
- Tint 1 tablespoon of remaining icing gray. Spread gray icing on elephant.
- Tint 1 to 2 tablespoons of remaining icing yellow and frost lion and giraffe.
- Tint remaining icing as desired for other animals, or spread orange icing on the camel and purple icing on the hippo.
- Pipe chocolate frosting generously over gorilla and cover with chocolate sprinkles, pressing them in place. Let dry.

---

5 **Add piped details.**
Using the star tip and different bright colors of ready-to-use decorating icing, pipe a thick border around each car. Pipe a coil of matching icing on 2 wheels for each car. Attach 2 wheels to each car with some icing, pressing lightly in place. (Wheels can extend just slightly below bottom of car.)

- Add matching decorations or words on each car as desired with star and small round tips.
- Pipe chocolate spots, mane and face on giraffe and lion as shown.

- Pipe black stripes, mane, tail and face on zebra and an ear and eye on elephant.
- Pipe lines of black icing to fill in ringmaster's top hat, pants and shoes. Draw a black bow tie and buttons as shown.
- Pipe yellow hair on clown using a star tip. Pipe blue and orange polka dots on clown's shirt and red stripes on clown's pants/skirt.
- Pipe chocolate, red, black and pink facial features on ringmaster, clown and remaining animals, using photo as a guide.

6 Make circus tent.

Tape 2 candy canes to 1 cookie stick, both hooks facing the same direction. Repeat with 2 more cookie sticks. Gather sticks together with all 6 hooks facing out. Tape the bottom of candy canes together. Push sticks into the center of cereal base for the "big top."

7 Put rest of bouquet together.

Place the ringmaster and clown in front of the candy canes, pushing sticks firmly into cereal base. Place a train car near outside edge, pushing sticks into base until wheels almost touch it. Place 1 or 2 animals behind car so they are visible. Repeat with remaining cars and animals around base, placing decorated sides facing out.

Celebration Suggestions...

Child's Birthday, Circus or Zoo Party, School Carnival, Children's "Cheer Up" or say, "Life is a circus!"

Hooray for the red, white and blue!
Celebrate America with these
star-studded sugar cookies featuring
colored sugars, ready-to-use
icings and sprinkles.

You will need:

- Container (Sample uses star-shaped cardboard box with lid, 9″ in diameter and 3″ deep.)
- Glossy acrylic paint (white, blue)
- Paintbrush
- Styrofoam
- Red shredded paper
- Perfectly Tender Sugar Cookie Dough (recipe on page 57)
- Cookie cutters (stars and hearts in several sizes, 1¾″ to 3″; 3½″ flag; 3½″ shooting star)
- Colored decorating sugars (red, blue)
- White sparkling sugar
- White lollipop sticks (4″, 6″, 8″)
- Toothpicks, optional
- Red, white and blue mixed sprinkles
- Ready-to-use decorating icing with star, leaf and small round tips (red, blue, white)

To Begin...

1 Prepare container. Press open end of star box against a sheet of foam that is at least 2″ thick. With a sharp knife, carefully cut out star, about ½″ inside outline. Trim as needed and check fit in box. Cover foam with foil; set aside. Paint outside and inner top edge of box white; let dry. Paint outside edges of box lid blue; let dry. Paint a second coat on box and lid; let dry completely. Press foil-covered foam into box and set box in blue lid. Scatter shredded paper on top.

2 Prepare cookies. Prepare Perfectly Tender Sugar Cookie Dough using recipe on page 57. (You will need a partial batch for this bouquet; use remaining dough for another bouquet.)

- For coiled cookies, roll a 1½″ to 2″ ball of dough between hands. Place dough on a lightly floured surface and roll with hands to make a "snake" about 12″ long. Sprinkle red and blue colored sugar on parchment paper and roll some of the snakes in colored sugar.

continued

Leave some snakes plain. Coil each snake and press end lightly to seal. If desired, gently roll edge of coils in white sparkling sugar.

- Transfer coils to ungreased or parchment paper-lined baking sheet, allowing space between cookies for sticks. Insert a stick into the bottom of each coil just past the middle, using a variety of 8″, 6″ and 4″ sticks.

- For cut-out cookies, roll out dough to a thickness of ⅜″. Cut these shapes with cookie cutters: 1 flag, 1 shooting star, 3 small stars, 6 larger stars, 2 small hearts and 2 larger hearts. Transfer cookies to ungreased or parchment paper-lined baking sheet, allowing space between cookies for sticks. Use 8″ sticks for shooting star, flag, 1 larger heart, 2 larger stars and 1 small star. Insert 6″ sticks into 1 small heart and 2 larger stars. Insert a toothpick into several of the smallest cookies. Use 4″ sticks for remaining cookies. Sprinkle tops of some cookies with colored sugars and/or white sparkling sugar before baking.

- Bake at 350° for 8 to 12 minutes or until just beginning to brown on the bottoms. Adjust time for size of cookies. Remove from oven and let cool on baking sheets for 2 minutes; transfer to waxed paper to cool completely.

3 Decorate cookies.

- Set aside several sugared, coiled cookies. On remaining plain and/or sugared cookies, use blue or red icing and tips of choice to pipe lines around the coils, in the creases or on top of coils.

- With white, blue or red icing and the star tip, outline several heart and star cookies. Outline or draw zig-zags on other cookies using the small round tip, including the shooting star. Add a dab of icing in the center of several cookies. Scatter red, white and blue sprinkles or white sparkling sugar over icing while wet, pressing lightly in place.
- Spread icing over several plain cut-out cookies; sprinkle with colored sugar. Let icings dry.

4 Put bouquet together.

Plan arrangement using photo as a guide. Begin with the tallest cookies at the back of the bouquet and work toward the front. Push sticks into foam base, moving shredded paper aside as needed. Place smallest cookies in front, pushing the sticks down until cookies almost rest on the red paper. Alternate the sugared and iced cookies and the colors and shapes until your arrangement looks balanced.

Variations:

- *Instead of using decorating icing, dip or drizzle cookies with melted vanilla candy coating or almond bark and immediately sprinkle colored sugars and sprinkles on top. Let dry.*
- *Wrap cookies in clear cellophane bags and tie them closed with patriotic ribbons.*

Celebration Suggestions...

Presidents' Day, Summer Picnic, Memorial Day, Flag Day, July 4th, Labor Day, Veterans Day or political events such as primaries or Election Day.

Decorated sugar cookies "float" on
an edible base made from frosted,
no-bake cereal treats, trimmed with
purchased shortbread cookies.

You will need:

- 1 (16.5 oz.) roll refrigerated sugar cookie dough (or a cookie recipe in this book)
- Flour and powdered sugar
- Cookie cutters (circles in two sizes, 2″ and 2¾″; 4″ double heart or cloud shape; 3″ flower or circle, 2¼″ butterfly)
- White lollipop sticks (4″, 6″, 8″)
- 9″ cardboard circle
- No-Bake Crispy Peanut Butter Treats (recipe on page 59 using butterscotch or white chocolate chips)

- 9″ round cake pan
- Ready-to-use chocolate and vanilla frostings
- Plastic piping bags fitted with star and small round tips.
- Ready-to-use decorating icing with star and round tips (blue*, yellow, red, purple, pink, green, white)
- ½ (10 oz.) box Lorna Doone shortbread cookies (about 20 cookies)

*You will need a full 6 ounces of blue decorating icing for "water."

To Begin...

1 Prepare cookies.

Soften refrigerated dough at room temperature. Divide dough into two portions and knead 1 tablespoon flour and 1 tablespoon powdered sugar into each portion until blended. Work with one portion at a time. Roll out dough to a thickness of ¼″ to ⅜″.

- Cut these shapes with cookie cutters: 4 (2″) circle heads, 2 (2¾″) circles (innertubes), 1 large flower or circle (sun), 2 double hearts or clouds, and 1 butterfly. Place similar-sized cookies on ungreased baking sheets, allowing space between cookies that need sticks.
- With knife, cut 1 x 2″ rectangles to make 2 or more hands/arms. Place on baking sheets and use

knife tip to press creases that look like fingers; trim "thumb" and fingers as desired.

- Insert 8″ sticks into sun and 1 cloud. Insert 6″ sticks into butterfly and remaining cloud.
- Bake cookies for 8 to 11 minutes or until just beginning to brown. Remove from oven and while large circles are still warm, cut out the center of each one with the 2″ cookie cutter to create the innertubes.

continued

Use the small circles you removed for beach balls. Quickly insert a 4″ stick into the bottom of 1 warm beach ball cookie. Transfer all cookies to waxed paper to cool completely.

2 Prepare base.

Cover the cardboard circle with plastic wrap; set aside. Line 9″ round cake pan with waxed paper and spray with nonstick cooking spray. Prepare 1½ batches of No-Bake Crispy Peanut Butter Treats with butterscotch or white chocolate chips, using the recipe on page 59. Press mixture into lined pan with buttered hands, packing firmly until level with top of pan; chill for at least 30 minutes.

3 Decorate cookies.

• Using photo as a guide, decorate medium round cookies into 4 different heads. Spoon chocolate frosting into a plastic piping bag with a star tip and make brown hair on several heads. Use the star or leaf tips on black, yellow or red icing to create hair on remaining heads. Use the small round tip on chocolate frosting and black icing to draw eyes on each face. Use small round tip on red icing to draw each mouth.

• Pipe thick lines of colored icing around each innertube. Add stripes or dots with contrasting icing.
• Frost "sun" cookie with yellow icing and add yellow piped edging with star tip. Use chocolate frosting with the small round tip to draw a face. Frost clouds with blue icing.

• Use icing in a variety of colors with the small round tip to decorate 2 beach balls as shown. Add a white dot in the middle.

- Decorate butterfly in a variety of icing colors using different tips.
- Spoon vanilla frosting into a plastic piping bag with a star tip (or purchase ready-to-use white icing in a tube). Outline clouds with thick lines as shown.

4 Decorate base.
Remove cereal base from pan and set it on prepared cardboard circle. Spread blue icing over top of cereal base to resemble water. Fasten the shortbread cookies to the side of the cereal base with a dab of blue frosting as shown, until outside edge of base is covered.

5 Put bouquet together.
- Set innertube cookies on blue "water." Use a knife or offset spatula to carve a slice into the cereal base in the center of each innertube. Make the cut ¾″ deep and wide enough to support the edge of a head cookie. Squeeze blue frosting into each cut and insert a head cookie into each one.
- Gently press the bottom of a hand/arm into the icing on each side of 1 or 2 heads, with hands reaching up in the air; use frosting to hold them in place as needed. Push the stick with the beach ball into the base near the hands/arms.
- Prop up the remaining beach ball with frosting.
- Insert sticks with the sun, clouds and butterfly cookies into the base behind other cookies, using photo as a guide.

Celebration Suggestions...

End of the School Year, Summer Birthday, Pool Party, Swim Team Party, Friendship or say "Make a splash in your new job", "Have a ball in retirement" or "You're a lifesaver!"

Monsters Love Cookies!

This arrangement can be made quickly
with purchased cookies and icing.
It's perfect for busy moms and
young party-goers.

You will need:

- Glass or clear plastic container (Sample uses a 5½" round glass cookie jar, 6" tall.)
- Styrofoam
- 1 (12 oz.) pkg. miniature chocolate chip cookies (about 1½" diameter, such as Famous Amos or Mini Chips Ahoy)
- 1 (16 oz.) pkg. chocolate chip cookies (2½" diameter)
- 4 oz. microwavable vanilla candy coating (or almond bark)

- 4 oz. microwavable chocolate candy coating (or almond bark)
- Wood craft sticks (about 12)
- Ready-to-use decorating icing (blue, white)
- Blue candy sprinkles (such as Betty Crocker brand)
- Ready-to-use black decorating icing with small round tip (or writing gel)

To Begin. . .

1 **Prepare container.** Purchase or cut a cylinder of foam about 2" smaller than diameter of cookie jar and 1" shorter. Wrap foam in foil and place in center of jar. To line container with cookies, slide miniature cookies, on edge, into cookie jar between foam and jar, tops facing out.

2 **Assemble cookies.** Follow package instructions to melt vanilla candy coating in a microwave, stirring until smooth.

- Spoon about 1 tablespoonful of melted candy on the center of the back side of 6 cookies. Press the end of a craft stick into melted candy with stick extending about 3" beyond edge of cookie. Press a second cookie on top of stick and candy; hold it in place for 10 seconds. Set the 6 sandwiched cookies on waxed paper until set, about 20 minutes.
- Repeat with chocolate candy coating to make 6 more cookie sandwiches.

3 Decorate cookies.

To make dipped cookies, reheat candy coating as needed until smooth or melt additional squares

- Holding one cookie sandwich over the measuring cup, spoon melted candy over half of cookie until coated, allowing excess to drip back into bowl. Scatter sprinkles on top of melted candy while wet, if desired. Repeat with 5 more cookie sandwiches, making both vanilla and chocolate dipped cookies. Let dry.

- Generously frost tops of remaining 6 cookie sandwiches with blue frosting. Scatter blue sprinkles over frosting, pressing gently to hold in place.

- Pipe 2 small mounds of white icing on each cookie for eyes, as shown. Add a dot of black icing to each eye. Flatten and smooth icing with fingertip as needed.
- Break 3 bite-size cookies in half. Press a cookie piece into blue frosting for each monster's mouth as shown; let dry.

4 Put bouquet together.

Plan arrangement. Alternate monsters and dipped cookies, starting at the back of the arrangement and working toward the front. Push sticks into foam base, making starter holes with toothpick if necessary. Break some miniature chocolate chip cookies into small pieces and scatter over top of foil.

Variation: Tasty cookie sandwiches may also be made from purchased oatmeal or peanut butter cookies.

Serving tip: The sticks make it very easy to dip cookies into cold milk!

Celebration Suggestions...

Child's Birthday, Preschool Party, "Blue" Party, Halloween, Dress-up Party or say, "You're my favorite cookie monster", "You're sweet and lovable" or "Me Love You!"

Delight Halloween guests with these
tasty cake balls decorated like small
jack-o-lanterns and ghosts. The
chocolate cookie sticks add
crunch and pizzazz.

You will need:

- Container (Sample uses round cardboard box, 6″ in diameter and 3″ deep.)
- Glossy orange acrylic paint
- Paintbrush
- Black stick-on scrapbooking letters (1″ tall)
- Orange tissue paper
- Chocolate Cake Balls (recipe on page 59)
- White cookie sticks (6″)
- Microwavable vanilla candy coating (or almond bark)
- Orange gel food coloring
- Ready-to-use decorating icing with small round and leaf tips (black, green)
- White lollipop sticks (4″)
- Sheet of styrofoam
- Chocolate Oreo Fun Stix (about 7)
- Candy corn

To Begin...

1 Prepare container. Paint the inside top edge and outside of box orange; let dry. Paint with a second coat if needed. Arrange and attach letters on front side of box as desired to say "Happy Halloween", "BOO!" or "Happy Haunting." Cut foam to fit container. Wrap foam in foil and cover with orange tissue paper; place into container.

2 Prepare cake balls. Prepare Chocolate Cake Balls using recipe on page 59. With hands, form dough into shapes as follows.

- Make 5 or more round or oblong balls for jack-o-lanterns. Cut several cookie sticks in half and insert a short stick into each jack-o-lantern shape. With a toothpick or table knife, make several creases in each ball to resemble real pumpkins.

- Make 3 or more ghost shapes, using fingers to create a wavy edge along bottom and mounding the center of each ghost a bit higher than the edges.

- Place all shapes on a baking sheet, allowing space between each one for sticks. Insert a full cookie stick into the bottom of each ghost shape.
- Freeze for at least 1 hour.

---

3 **Coat cake balls with melted vanilla candy coating.** Follow package instructions to melt 6 ounces of vanilla candy coating in a glass measuring cup in the microwave; stir until smooth and creamy.

- Holding ghost shape on a fork over the measuring cup, spoon white candy coating over each ghost to cover the front side. Gently tap off excess coating on the side of bowl. Set ghosts on waxed paper to dry. When coating is dry, turn ghosts over and spread more white candy coating over back sides with a spoon; let dry.

- Add a generous amount of orange gel food coloring to remaining melted candy coating and stir until color reaches desired intensity. Reheat coating as needed to keep it melted and smooth. Using the same method, spoon melted orange coating over each pumpkin shape, turning cake ball until well covered. Set pumpkins on waxed paper to dry.

Tip: Stir ½ teaspoon vegetable oil into melted candy if it sets up too fast on the frozen cake balls.

Note: For best results, use gel food coloring with melted candy coating, not liquid food coloring.

4 Add decorations to shapes.

- Use black decorating icing with a small round tip to draw eyes, nose and mouth on pumpkins to create different jack-o-lantern faces. Draw black eyes and an optional mouth on each ghost. After icing is slightly set, use a fingertip to flatten points of icing as needed.

- Push ends of pumpkin sticks into a sheet of Styrofoam. Use green decorating icing with a leaf tip to make a stem and leaf on top of each jack-o-lantern.

Change to a small round tip to make the curling green vines. Let dry.

5 Put bouquet together.

Plan arrangement using the photo as a guide. Insert sticks into foam base, making starter holes with toothpick as needed. Place tall ghosts toward the back and center; place shorter jack-o-lanterns toward the front. Be sure to balance the weight of bouquet so it won't tip. Finally, push the lollipop sticks into the foam behind the ghosts. Slide an Oreo Fun Stix down over each lollipop stick. Break off Stix tops as desired to stagger the height of the brown "fence", making it look spooky. Scatter candy corn over tissue paper base.

Celebration Suggestions...

Halloween, Trick or Treating, Spooky Slumber Party or say, "Be brave!" or "Still waiting for the great pumpkin."

Create an edible basket from no-bake cereal treats covered in vanilla sandwich cookies. Fill it with purchased oatmeal cookies you decorate easily with colorful icing.

You will need:

- Base (Sample uses a 12″ cardboard circle covered in parchment paper and food-safe green cellophane.)
- Deep plastic storage container (about 4½ x 6″)
- No-Bake Crispy Peanut Butter Treats (recipe on page 59 using butterscotch chips)
- Vienna Fingers cream-filled sandwich cookies (about 16 cookies)
- Ready-to-use decorating icing (white, red, purple, green, yellow, black, orange)
- Purchased 2¾″ round oatmeal or sugar cookies (12 to 16 cookies)
- Decorating tips (small round, star)
- Writing icing or gel
- Toothpicks

To Begin...

1 **Prepare cardboard base.**
Cut a 12″ circle from several layers of cardboard. Cover with parchment paper or foil and cellophane or plastic wrap, taping it to back side.

2 **Prepare and mold the crispy treat base.**
Line the plastic container with aluminum foil, leaving an overhang. Coat foil with nonstick cooking spray and set aside. Prepare No-Bake Crispy Peanut Butter Treats with butterscotch chips using the recipe on page 59. Press mixture firmly into prepared container with buttered hands. Chill in freezer for about 30 minutes.

3 **Make the edible basket.**
Pull up on foil to remove cereal base from plastic container. Peel off foil. Set cereal base in the center of prepared cardboard base. Apply some icing to the back side of a Vienna Finger cookie. Press cookie against the side of the cereal base as shown. Repeat with remaining cookies until outside edge of cereal base is covered. Let icing dry.

4 Decorate cookies.

Using the photo as a guide, apply colored icing on top of each oatmeal cookie to create a fruit, vegetable or leaf shape as follows. Let icing dry before assembling bouquet.

- *Pears, pumpkins, apples, plums, tomatoes and leaves:* Squeeze a generous amount of colored icing on center of cookie; spread with a knife or offset spatula to make the correct shape. Mix colors as desired for leaves. Use a toothpick to draw details, such as pumpkin or leaf lines. Go over them with writing icing or gel, if desired. Add green or black stems/leaves to fruits and vegetables using a small round tip.

- *Cherries or grapes:* Use the large round tip on the icing tube (or a star tip) to make small balls, clustering them as shown. Flatten as needed with a toothpick or fingertip. Add green icing stems using a small round tip or writing icing.

- *Ear of corn:* Use a small round tip to make the outline of the ear of corn. Make small balls of yellow icing to look like the kernels. Fill in the leaves, adding green as desired.

5 Put bouquet together.

Arrange fruit and vegetable cookies in the edible basket, propping up each cookie with a toothpick poked into the cereal base. Arrange leaf cookies on cardboard base around basket. After cookies are removed, cut and serve the cereal treat base.

Variations:

- *Make a basket filled with summer flowers. Decorate each cookie to look like a different flower and arrange an assortment of them in the edible basket. It's a perfect summertime centerpiece since you don't have to turn on your oven.*
- *Press the cereal base into a small wheelbarrow container and arrange cookies within it. Or, omit the cereal base and fill wheelbarrow with food-safe shredded paper and simply set the decorated cookies inside.*

Celebration Suggestions...

Thanksgiving, Fall Harvest, First Day of Autumn, Fall Birthday or say, "Thanks for all you've done."

Thanksgiving Gobbler

Entertain everyone with this
sweet turkey made with purchased
wafer cookies and mini
chocolate chip cookies attached
to a chocolate cereal base.

You will need:

- No-Bake Crispy Peanut Butter Treats (recipe on page 59 using chocolate chips)
- 36 to 40 wafer cookies (vanilla, chocolate, strawberry)
- 20 to 24 miniature chocolate chip cookies
- 1 Nutter Butter cookie (available in a snack size four-pack)

- 1 candy corn
- 2 miniature brown M&M candies
- White ready-to-use decorating icing
- Red writing icing (not gel)
- Toothpicks (Flat ones work best.)
- Serving plate (11″ to 12″)
- Additional candy corn, optional

To Begin...

1 **Prepare and mold the crispy treat base.**
Prepare No-Bake Crispy Peanut Butter Treats with chocolate chips using the recipe on page 59. With buttered hands, mold mixture on waxed paper to create a slightly oval mound about 6″ long and 4″ high in the center. Pack firmly. Chill in freezer for about 30 minutes.

2 **Prepare cookies.**
- Insert a toothpick into the end of each wafer cookie, at least 1″ deep. Make 12 to 14 of each color.
- Decorate the turkey's head on the Nutter Butter cookie. Attach the brown M&M eyes with a drop of white icing. Cut off the yellow portion of a candy corn and attach the cut end beneath eyes with icing to make the beak. Use red or pink writing icing to draw a waddle and outline the cookie, if desired. Let icing dry.

3 Assemble head and neck.

Cut 1 vanilla wafer cookie in half. Insert a toothpick half into the end of each cookie piece for turkey's neck. Press toothpicks into a piece of Styrofoam, placing cookies side by side and making cut edges even on top for the neck. Attach turkey's head to top of neck with white icing; let dry.

4 Attach turkey's tail feathers and head.

Remove waxed paper from cereal base and transfer base to a serving plate. Starting at the top of cereal base, just past the center point, gently push toothpicks with wafer cookies into base. Alternate colors randomly and fan the cookies to look like feathers as shown. Fill the entire back side of turkey. Remove neck/head from foam and gently push toothpicks on neck/head into center of cereal base as shown.

5 Attach chest feathers.

Attach chocolate chip cookies over the remaining visible cereal base with white icing. Overlap and use pieces of cookies as needed to resemble feathers and cover base. Let dry.

6 Garnish plate.

If desired, arrange candy corn around base of turkey.

Celebration Suggestions...

Thanksgiving, Child's Party or use this centerpiece as a gag gift to say, "Gobble Up!", "Birds of a feather... " or "From one turkey to another!"

Oh Christmas Tree

Celebrate the season with
this tree covered with faux
peppermint candies. They're
really pinwheel cookies
sandwiched with
peppermint frosting.

You will need:

- Perfectly Tender Sugar Cookie Dough (recipe on page 57)
- Red gel or paste food coloring
- Clear plastic wrap
- 2½″ star cookie cutter
- Yellow decorating sugar
- Toothpick
- Buttercream Frosting (recipe on page 60)
- 7 yards sheer white ribbon (¼″ wide)
- Small artificial Christmas tree (Sample tree is 22″ tall.)
- Wire ornament hooks or craft wire bent into "S" shapes

To Begin...

1 Prepare cookie dough.

Prepare Perfectly Tender Sugar Cookie Dough using recipe on page 57).

- Divide dough in half. Tint 1 portion red using a generous amount of food coloring; work it through dough with hands while wearing plastic gloves. Leave remaining dough white.
- Divide each portion in half to make two red and two white portions. Flatten each portion of dough into a 4 x 6″ rectangular disk; wrap in plastic and refrigerate for 2 hours.

2 Roll out dough

- Roll one portion of white dough into a rectangular layer, about 7 x 10″ and ¼″ to ⅜″ thick. From one end of the rectangle, cut out a star cookie and place it on ungreased or parchment paper-lined baking sheet. Insert a toothpick into one edge. Sprinkle star with yellow sugar; set aside.
- Roll red dough into a layer the same size and shape as the white dough. Stack and lightly press the two

layers together; trim uneven edges.

- Beginning at one long edge, roll layered dough into a log, jelly roll style. Chill for 30 minutes. Use this log roll to cut largest cookies.

- To make medium and small cookies, roll remaining portions of white and red dough into 2 rectangular layers, about 5 x 14" each. Use a pizza cutter to cut both rectangles in half crosswise (to make four 5 x 7" pieces). Stack 1 red layer on 1 white layer. Stack remaining white layer on remaining red layer. Press layers together lightly with hands. Trim uneven edges as needed. Roll dough into 2 fat logs from long edge as before. Chill for 30 minutes.

3 Slice, flatten and bake cookies.

- Make the medium and small cookies first. Slice half of each dough log into rounds ½" thick and 1¼" in diameter. Place on prepared baking sheet (with star cookie) and flatten each slice to ¼" thickness with the bottom of a drinking glass dipped in sugar.

- To make smaller cookies, unroll remainder of each log partway and trim off flat section. Cut slices from remaining log and flatten as before. Re-roll trimmed-off section, cut slices and flatten to make the smallest cookies.

- Using remaining large log of red and white dough, slice and flatten large cookies on prepared baking sheet. (For smaller cookies, unroll partway and cut as directed for small cookies above.)
- Bake at 350° for 8 to 12 minutes, depending on size, until just beginning to brown on bottoms. Remove from oven and let cool on baking sheets for 2 minutes; transfer to waxed paper to cool completely.

4 Prepare frosting and sandwich cookies together.

Prepare Buttercream Frosting with peppermint extract using recipe on page 60. Spread frosting on the bottom side of half the cookies. Top with matching cookies, gently pressing to form a sandwich.

5 Wrap cookies.

Cut 2 (5″) pieces of ribbon for each cookie. Tear off 5″ to 7″ of plastic wrap for each cookie. Wrap each cookie in plastic wrap, gather ends and tie snugly with ribbon. Trim ends of plastic wrap and ribbon with scissors to approximately 1″; fluff out plastic.

6 Assemble tree.

Slide one end of a wire ornament or "S" hook under the ribbon at one end of each cookie. Hang other end of hook over tree branches as desired, placing larger cookies near the bottom of tree and smaller cookies at the top. Tie 12″ of ribbon into a bow around toothpick under star cookie. Slide toothpick into top of tree.

Variations:
- *In place of the tree, set an artificial evergreen wreath or spray on your holiday table and tuck the wrapped cookies among the branches.*
- *Shred green and silver metallic tissue and place in a glass candy bowl. Arrange wrapped cookies in bowl.*

Celebration Suggestions...

Christmas, Holiday Hostess Gift, Dorm Room Christmas Cheer, Final Exams Treat, Holiday Bazaar or Open House.

Chocolate Posy Perfection

These pretty paper flowers have
edible centers made from
chocolate cake balls coated
in almond bark.

You will need:

- Container (Sample uses a ceramic vase, 3¾″ in diameter and 4″ tall.)
- Styrofoam
- Scrapbooking paper or other decorative paper
- Flower-shaped cookie cutters (graduated sizes and shapes from 1″ to 3½″)
- Push pin
- Chocolate Cake Balls (recipe on page 59)
- Toothpicks

- 8 to 10 oz. white almond bark
- 1 tsp. vegetable oil
- Pink gel food coloring, optional
- White or green lollipop sticks (4″, 6″, 8″)
- Sugar sprinkles (pink, blue, green)
- Chocolate candy sprinkles
- Sheet of Styrofoam
- Ivory shredded paper
- Green tissue paper, optional

To Begin...

1 Prepare container.

Cut foam to fit into vase snugly. Wrap with foil and place into vase.

2 Prepare paper flowers.

- Choose several coordinating paper colors and patterns. Trace around cookie cutters, making different sizes of flowers on each paper. Cut out smaller circles or stars for flower centers. If paper has printed flower shapes, cut out a variety of these.

- Layer 2 or 3 paper shapes together to create each flower, with largest pieces on the bottom. Mix and match papers and shapes. Make enough sets for 16 to 20 cake balls. With a push pin, poke a starter hole in the center of each paper piece; set aside.

3 Prepare cake balls.

Prepare Chocolate Cake Balls using recipe on page 59. Roll dough into 16 to 20 small balls, ¾″ to 1¼″ in diameter. Place balls on a baking sheet, poke a toothpick into each one and freeze for at least 1 hour.

4 Prepare coating and decorate cake balls.

- Remove each toothpick and insert a lollipop stem in its place. Place 5 balls on 8″ sticks, at least 3 balls on 6″ sticks and remaining balls on 4″ sticks.

- In a large microwave-safe measuring cup, melt almond bark for 60 seconds. Add oil, stir and cook again as needed until smooth. Tint a portion of the melted bark with pink food coloring, if desired. Hold a cake ball over the measuring cup and spoon melted bark over it until coated, rotating ball and letting excess drip back into cup.

- Sprinkle wet bark with colored sugar or candy sprinkles. Push end of stick into a sheet of Styrofoam covered with waxed paper to let coating dry.

5 Assemble flowers.
Push the end of a cake ball stem into each set of paper flowers, gently enlarging the starter holes one layer at a time. Slide flowers up to base of cake ball. Rotate the paper layers as desired.

6 Arrange flowers in container.
Plan arrangement using photo as a guide. Push stems of tallest flowers into foam base near the center. Arrange 6″ flowers around those, with the shortest ones around outer edges. Before completing bouquet, arrange shredded paper between stems to cover foil base.

Celebration Suggestions...

Mother's Day, Valentine's Day, Bridal Shower, Congratulations, Job Promotion, Recuperation, Friendship, Good Luck, or say, "It's been a ball!"

Recipes and Baking Tips

Lemon Sugar Cookie Dough
Makes about 36 cookies

½ C. butter-flavored shortening
1 C. sugar
1 egg
1½ tsp. lemon flavoring (or orange, vanilla or almond extract)
½ tsp. butter flavoring

2 tsp. lemon juice
¼ C. milk
3 C. flour, divided
½ tsp. baking powder
½ tsp. baking soda
½ tsp. salt
½ tsp. ground nutmeg, optional

In a large mixing bowl, beat together shortening and sugar on medium speed. Add egg and beat until fluffy. Add extract of choice, butter flavoring and lemon juice, mixing until blended. Stir in milk. In a separate bowl, stir together 2¾ cups flour, baking powder, baking soda, salt and nutmeg, if desired. Add dry ingredients to creamed mixture and mix well. Stir in additional ¼ cup flour with a wooden spoon to make a soft dough. Cover and chill for at least 1 hour. Then follow cutting and baking instructions on page 58, using lightly greased or parchment paper-lined baking sheets.

Sweet Cut-Out Sugar Cookie Dough
Makes 24 to 36 cookies

¾ C. butter or margarine, softened
1¼ C. sugar
1 egg

2 tsp. vanilla or almond extract
2½ C. flour
½ tsp. salt

In a large mixing bowl, beat together butter, sugar and egg on high speed until fluffy, about 3 minutes. Blend in vanilla. In a separate bowl, stir together flour and salt. Add dry ingredients to creamed mixture and stir well with a wooden spoon until dough comes together. Use hands as needed to make smooth, stiff dough. If desired, divide dough into several portions and shape each one into a flat disk. Cover and chill for 2 to 3 hours or until firm enough to roll. Then follow cutting and baking instructions on page 58, using ungreased baking sheets.

Perfectly Tender Sugar Cookie Dough
Makes 24 to 36 cookies

This dough is soft but easy to handle. It works well for cookies that are coiled, folded or stacked, such as the pinwheel variations in this book.

¾ C. butter, softened
3 oz. cream cheese, softened
1 C. sugar
1 egg
1 tsp. clear vanilla or
  almond extract

2¾ C. flour
1 tsp. baking powder
¼ tsp. salt

In a large mixing bowl, cream butter, cream cheese and sugar on medium speed until fluffy. Beat in egg and vanilla until well blended. In a separate bowl, stir together flour, baking powder and salt. Add dry ingredients to creamed mixture and stir with a wooden spoon until flour mixture is incorporated and soft dough forms. If desired, divide dough into several portions and add color. Cover and chill for 2 hours. Then follow cutting and baking instructions in individual recipes, using ungreased or parchment paper-lined baking sheets.

Chocolate Cut-Out Cookie Dough
Makes 24 to 36 cookies

1 C. butter, softened
¾ C. sugar
2 egg yolks
1 tsp. vanilla extract

1¾ C. flour
½ C. unsweetened cocoa
  powder
¼ tsp. salt

In a large mixing bowl, beat together butter and sugar for 3 to 4 minutes, until creamed and fluffy. Add egg yolks and vanilla; beat until blended. In a separate bowl, stir together flour, cocoa powder and salt. Gradually add flour mixture to creamed mixture, beating after each addition and working with hands if necessary until dough comes together. Cover and chill for at least 1 hour. Then follow rolling, cutting and baking instructions on page 58, using lightly greased or parchment paper-lined baking sheets.

General Cutting, Baking and Stem Instructions for all Cut-Out Cookies

Preheat oven to 350°. Divide dough and work with one portion at a time. Roll out dough to a thickness of ¼″ to ½″ on a lightly floured surface. Thickness will depend on style of bouquet being made; see bouquet instructions. Prepare baking sheets as directed in recipes. Cut into desired shapes and space cookies evenly on a shiny baking sheet, leaving room for the sticks. Insert a lollipop or cookie stick into one edge of each cookie, twisting it gently to keep stick inside dough. Sticks should be inserted 1″ to 2½″, depending on cookie size. (Larger or heavier cookies may need 2 sticks for good support.) Bake for 8 to 14 minutes, adjusting time for size and thickness. Cool cookies on baking sheets for about 2 minutes before removing to waxed paper to cool completely.

Rolling Tips

- Divide dough into portions that are easy to handle.
- Chilled dough is easier to roll out, but if dough becomes very stiff when chilled, let it warm up slightly before rolling.
- Form dough into a flat disk before rolling out on a lightly floured board.
- Roll out cookie dough effortlessly by taping a large piece of floured canvas to the countertop. Cover a wooden rolling pin with a cloth pastry sleeve and flour it well before use.
- After cutting out cookie shapes, remove dough scraps and set aside. Do all first rollings and cuttings; then combine scraps to re-roll and cut additional shapes. Cookies become slightly drier and tougher with each re-rolling.
- For best results, cookies must be cut thick enough so sticks can be inserted into dough. Alternatively, layer 2 thin cookies together with the stick pressed between them.

Baking Tips

- Bake cookies on the center rack in a preheated oven.
- Place cookies of similar size and thickness on the same baking sheet for even baking.
- If cookies puff up during baking, flatten the tops of hot cookies with a smooth spatula before cooling and decorating.
- Dough can be refrigerated overnight or frozen. Dough can also be rolled, cut and frozen to be baked later, or baked and frozen before frosting. Store baked cookies in an airtight container.
- Decorate cookies the same day you assemble and serve bouquet for freshest results.

No-Bake Crispy Peanut Butter Treats
Use this mixture for edible bases

1 C. butterscotch chips
  (or chocolate chips)

½ C. peanut butter
4 C. crisp rice cereal

In a large microwave-safe bowl, combine butterscotch chips and peanut butter. Microwave on high for 60 seconds. Stir and cook again until chips melt and mixture is blended and smooth. Add rice cereal and stir until well coated. Press into prepared pan or mold with hands to desired shape. Chill in refrigerator or freezer for at least 30 minutes before use.

Chocolate Cake Balls
Makes about 20 small balls or 8 to 10 larger shapes

3 C. crumbled chocolate
  cake scraps*
3 T. powdered sugar
1½ T. unsweetened cocoa
  powder

3 T. miniature chocolate chips
  or chopped almonds, optional
3 to 4 T. Amaretto-flavored
  liquid coffee creamer
  (or other flavor)

In a large bowl, combine crumbled cake, powdered sugar and cocoa powder; mix well. Stir in miniature chocolate chips, if desired. Add liquid coffee creamer, 1 tablespoon at a time, and mix with a spoon until a soft, mushy dough forms. Use hands to roll small balls or make shapes with the cake mixture. Place shapes on a baking sheet and press a toothpick into each one. Freeze cake balls for at least 1 hour. Remove toothpick and insert desired lollipop or cookie sticks. Coat chilled cake balls in melted almond bark or candy coating with additional decorations as directed in bouquet instructions.

If using white cake, use 3 tablespoons cocoa powder.

Royal Cookie Icing

2 C. powdered sugar
1½ T. meringue powder
½ tsp. clear vanilla extract

3 T. warm water
Gel food coloring

In a medium mixing bowl, beat together powdered sugar, meringue powder, vanilla and water to reach a smooth spreading consistency, 4 to 5 minutes. Use the back of a spoon or offset spatula to spread icing over cookies. Tap iced cookies gently on counter to smooth out icing as needed. Thin with a little warm water as needed to get a smooth shiny surface.

Buttercream Frosting

½ C. butter or margarine,
    softened
3¾ C. powdered sugar
Pinch of salt

2 tsp. clear vanilla extract
    (or lemon flavoring or
    peppermint extract)
3 T. milk

In a medium bowl, combine butter, powdered sugar and salt; beat well with electric mixer or wire whisk. Stir in vanilla and milk; beat until smooth. If frosting is too thick, add additional milk, a little at a time, until desired consistency is reached.

To Apply Icing or Frosting

Use the back of a spoon or an offset spatula to nudge icing or frosting toward cookie edges. A toothpick can be used to move it into small areas. Be sure the base coat of icing is dry before applying contrasting details.

To Pipe on Icing or Frosting

Thicken prepared icing or frosting by adding more powdered sugar, a spoonful at a time. Mix well until piping consistency is reached. Spoon thickened icing into a plastic piping bag with tip or a durable zippered plastic bag. Push mixture into one corner of the zippered bag. Snip off a small piece of the corner with scissors. Twist bag above the icing and squeeze evenly to pipe icing out of the hole in the bag. Be sure base icing is dry to the touch before piping on details. Points of partially set icing can be pressed in place with a light touch from your fingertip.

Glazing Cookies for Storage

To keep unfrosted cookies fresh for up to 2 weeks, brush baked, cooled cookies with a glaze. Mix together ½ cup powdered sugar, 1 teaspoon light corn syrup and 2 teaspoons warm water. Stir well and brush glaze over one side of cookies. Let dry on waxed paper for 1 hour. Turn cookies over and brush second side. Let dry completely before storing or decorating. Glazed cookies can be frozen in an airtight container and decorated later.